NAPKIN
FOLDING

AND TABLE DECORATIONS

NAPKIN
FOLDING
AND TABLE DECORATIONS

BRIDGET JONES AND MADELEINE BREHAUT

Special photography by James Duncan

HERMES
HOUSE

This Paperback edition published by
Hermes House an imprint of Anness Publishing Limited
Hermes House 88-89 Blackfriars Road
London SE1 8HA

A CIP catalogue record for this book is available from the British Library

ISBN 1 84038 719 X

Publisher: Joanna Lorenz
Project Editor: Jennifer Jones
Assistant Editor: Charles Moxham
Designer: Adrian Morris
Special Photography: James Duncan
Stylist: Madeleine Brehaut
Illustrator: Kate Simunek

Printed and bound in Singapore

© Anness Publishing Limited 1994 1998
Updated © 2000
1 3 5 7 9 10 8 6 4 2

CONTENTS

NAPKIN ART

*C*risp, *freshly laundered napkins are an essential feature of every well-set table. They may be pressed in large, plain squares and laid at each place with the minimum of fuss and for the maximum effect. Alternatively, they may be* folded in a variety of ways to complement the food, table layout and occasion. Try some of the ideas in the following pages and use them as a source of inspiration for developing your own individual napkin art.*

PERFECT NAPKINS

Regardless of the simplicity of the meal, fabric napkins must be spotlessly clean and well pressed.

❖ Plain white linen napkins may be embroidered by hand or by machine with a monogram of your initials. This may be surrounded by a wreath of leaves or some other decorative embroidery. Fold monogrammed napkins very simply to display the embroidery.

❖ Press embroidered napkins on the wrong side to make the pattern stand out attractively.

❖ Decorative napkins, trimmed with embroidery or lace or with a prominent self pattern, should be folded very simply; plain fabric napkins or those with a small decorative border are more suitable for elaborate folding.

NAPKINS FOR BUFFETS

If you are preparing a buffet for a comparatively small number, that is, under fifteen guests, then it is a good idea to use linen napkins if possible. The fabrics do not have to be the same and a virtue can be made of their differences by combining contrasting colours or patterns in an attractive arrangement.

❖ For larger gatherings or when there are lots of children around, it is an advantage to have lots of spare paper napkins to deal with any spills. Bear in mind that guests rarely retain their napkins after the main course and many may take a second for dessert.

❖ Elaborate folding methods are not used for buffet presentation as the emphasis is mainly on the practicalities of carrying a plate, napkin and cutlery (flatware). There are a number of standard options for placing napkins.

❖ Roll a knife and fork in a napkin. If the number of guests is small and space on the buffet table limited, the cutlery and napkins may be fanned out attractively, near the plates. It is often more practical to pile them in a basket, or two, and place them near the plates or on a separate side table with condiments or bread. Do not roll cutlery for

---

Paper Napkins

Paper napkins are more practical than fabric ones for parties. Choose those that are large, absorbent and fairly thick; the thin, small paper napkins that disintegrate easily are more hindrance than help. The exception to this rule is Japanese paper napkins.

BRIGHT PAPER NAPKINS For fun parties use a selection of different coloured paper napkins: pastels or primary colours both work well. Fold them in half, then overlap them in a large basket and fold one napkin into a water lily shape for the centre of the arrangement.

Paper napkins are a practical option for informal barbecues, especially when sticky spareribs and other finger foods are served. When laying a garden table, allow two or three different coloured napkins for each place setting. They may be fanned out simply or pairs of contrasting colours used double for folding shapes such as a water lily or roll-top design.

JAPANESE PAPER NAPKINS Look out for fine paper napkins which are very thin but quite strong. They are often delicately patterned and may be round or square, with fluted or gilded edges. As well as being used on their own, they may be used in conjunction with linen napkins for courses which are eaten with the fingers as part of a formal meal, especially when finger bowls are provided. Fold them attractively with the linen napkins, then clear the paper napkins away after they have been used.

A tartan bow holds a neatly rolled napkin and spoon for a dessert course.

dessert in the napkin; this should be offered separately.

❖ Stack a napkin on each plate.

❖ Fold the napkins in half diagonally to make triangles and overlap these on one side of the buffet table.

❖ Roll the napkins and stand them in a wide jug or arrange them in a basket.

TIPS FOR SUCCESSFUL FOLDING

For folding purposes, heavy linen is best, as it becomes firm and crisp when starched. Plain dinner napkins measuring 45–50 cm/18–20 in square, or more, are best and are essential for many complicated folding techniques.

❖ The napkins must be cut square and the fabric must be cut straight on the weave so that the napkins will not pull out of shape easily.

❖ Linen should be washed, starched with traditional starch (spray starch will not give a sufficiently crisp finish) and ironed while damp. When ironing, gently pull the napkins back into shape if necessary to ensure they are perfectly square again.

❖ It is best to iron napkins on a large surface; an ironing board can be too narrow when pressing large napkins. Protect the surface with a folded thick

towel, which should be covered with a piece of plain white cotton.

❖ Dampen napkins which have dried before ironing. Traditional starch may be mixed and sprayed on linen using a clean plant spray. Allow it to soak into

the fabric for a minute or so before ironing for best results.

When folding napkins into complicated shapes, press each fold individually for best results. Soft folds should not be pressed.

SIMPLE PRESENTATION

To form a neat square, press the napkin, making sure all the corners are perfectly square. Fold it into quarters, pressing each fold. A large quarter-folded napkin may be laid square between the cutlery (flatware) at each place or it may be turned by ninety degrees. This is fine on large tables.

❖ To make a simple triangle, fold the square in half diagonally and press the resulting triangle neatly. Lay the triangular-folded napkin on a side plate, with the long side nearest the place setting. The triangle may also be laid on top of a plate in the middle of the setting.

❖ For a simple oblong, fold a square napkin in half again. This is an ideal way of displaying a decorative corner on the napkin. Plain napkins may be folded and pressed into quarters, then the sides folded underneath and pressed to make an oblong shape. Lay the hemmed edge on the short side at the bottom of the place setting.

❖ Rolled napkins may be kept in place with napkin rings or tied with ribbon or cord. If the napkins are rolled carefully and laid with the end underneath, they will usually sit quite neatly.

Pure & Simple

As its name suggests, this design is quickly arranged and pleasing to the eye. The outcome is particularly elegant if a 'lace' edged napkin is used.

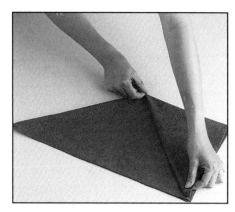

1 Start with the corners of the napkin top and bottom in the form of a diamond. Fold the corner nearest to you up to meet the top point. With a finger at the centre bottom, fold the bottom left point up to the top point.

2 Fold the right bottom point up to meet the top point.

3 Turn the napkin over, keeping the open corners furthest from you. Fold the bottom point a third of the way up the napkin.

4 Carefully tuck both sides under the napkin.

Wave

The elegant lines of rippling edges are shown to best effect when folded on a blue or green napkin.

1 Fold the top edge of the napkin down to the bottom. Pick up the top layer at the bottom right point and bring the corner over to meet the bottom left, forming a large triangle.

2 Carefully turn the napkin over. Lift the top layer of the bottom right corner and bring it over to the bottom left, to form a matching triangle on this side.

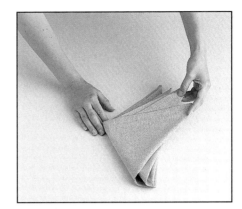

3 Pick up the two right-hand points and bring them over to the left, slightly splaying all four points of the napkin.

4 Roll under a little of the right-hand edge at a slight angle and pinch to finish.

Spreading Fan

An elegant yet simple design that is suitable for all occasions.

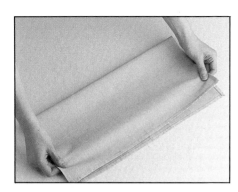  

1 Fold up the edge nearest to you to meet the top edge.

2 Rotate the napkin so that the folded edge is on your right. Make equal-sized accordian pleats all the way up to the top of the napkin, starting with the edge nearest to you.

3 Insert the napkin into the ring, or tie with ribbon or cord and spread out the pleats.

Candle

This festive fold is the perfect christmas touch. Green or red napkins are particularly suitable.

1 Starting with the corners of the open napkin top and bottom in the form of a diamond, fold the corner nearest to you to meet the top point. Next fold the bottom edge up a short way to form a narrow hem.

2 Hold the hem firmly, and carefully turn over the napkin so that the long folded edge is to your right. Then roll up the napkin beginning from the bottom point and stopping short of the small top tail.

3 Turn the candle round so that the tail now faces you and tuck the tail into the band to secure the roll.

4 Tuck the top loose point into the roll and form a flame shape with the second loose point underneath.

Place Mat

A large, square, cloth napkin can be used as a pretty place mat.

1 Fold the four corners into the centre.

2 Place a hand over the middle to hold the corners in position and turn the napkin over.

3 Fold all four corners of the napkin into the centre again and carefully turn the napkin over for a second time.

4 Fold each centre corner back to meet the outside corner, and press.

Buffet Parcel

While balancing a plate in one hand this tidy fold allows you to carry napkin and cutlery at a pinch.

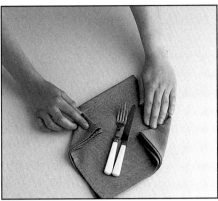

1 Fold the napkin into quarters. Place a knife and fork in the centre of the square. Fold in the two side points to form two small triangles.

2 Bring the two side folds over the cutlery to cover it completely.

3 Secure the bundle with ribbon tied in a bow.

Lover's Knot

This simple design lends a romantic touch to a candle-lit dinner or anniversary breakfast.

1 Starting with the corners of the open napkin top and bottom in the form of a diamond, fold the top point down to the bottom point.

2 Starting from the bottom point, make accordion pleats up to the top edge.

3 With the first pleat facing away from you, fold the right point over the left one and tuck back through the loop created to form a loose but tidy knot.

Festival

Boldly fanning out, Festival is well suited to more colourful napkins and lively occasions.

1 With the corners of the open napkin top and bottom in the form of a diamond, fold the corner nearest to you up to meet the top point.

2 Make accordion pleats all the way across the napkin starting from the bottom edge, gathering each pleat under the last.

3 Fold the pleated napkin in half from left to right. Pinch at the fold to hold the shape and lay out on the plate.

Iris in a Glass

This design can create a very striking display if folded with a large, colourful napkin.

Opposite: Iris in a Glass.

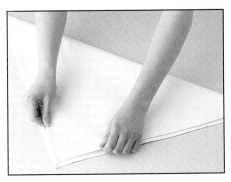

1 Starting with the corners of the open napkin top and bottom in the form of a diamond, bring the point nearest to you up to the top point to form a triangle.

2 With a finger at the centre of the fold line, fold up the two corners nearest to you so they are level with the centre top point and slightly to each side of it.

3 Fold the newly formed bottom point part-way up towards the top point, as shown.

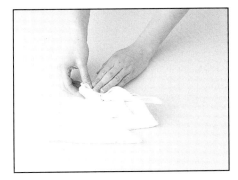

4 Make accordian pleats across the napkin from left to right. Position the napkin in the glass and fan out the petals of the iris.

Fan on a Plate

Use a carefully starched linen napkin for this elegant design.

1 Fold the napkin in half to form a rectangle. Starting at the edge nearest to you, make eight fairly small, accordian pleats. Press each pleat as you work. Use two-thirds of the rectangle for pleating.

2 Fold the napkin in half so that the two edges meet on the left and the pleats are on the outside bottom edge.

3 Fold the top edge — the edge furthest away from you — down to make a small band. Then bring top left corner down to the bottom right and tuck it under the pleats. Turn the napkins so that it stands on the right edge. Then, holding the bottom with one hand, fan out the pleats.

Wings

This light-hearted design works best with a stiff cotton napkin and is quick to capture the imagination of young children.

1 Fold the bottom and top edges of the open napkin into the centre. Bring the bottom fold up to the top.

2 Fold in the left side by a third.

3 Fold this side back on itself to align with the outside edge again.

4 Repeat the process with the right side. Lift the top layers on both sides and curl them back under into their own folds to form the wings.

Flickering Flames

An effective yet straightforward design which enhances the glassware on your table. You need two lightweight fringed cloth or paper napkins.

1 Place the two napkins one on top of the other with all edges aligned. Fold up the edges nearest to you to meet the top edges.

2 Fold the napkin in half again by bringing the right edges over to the left edges.

3 Turn the napkin round, placing the open corners away from you, and fold the bottom corner about a third of the way up the napkin.

4 Make accordion pleats across the napkin starting from the left point.

5 Firmly holding the bottom, gently open out the layers to form the flames and place in glass to finish.

Candy Cane

For this simple but effective design you will need two different-coloured cloth or paper napkins of the same size.

1 Lay one open napkin on top of the other. Place the top one slightly higher and to the left of the bottom one leaving a small v-shaped border of contrasting colour visible.

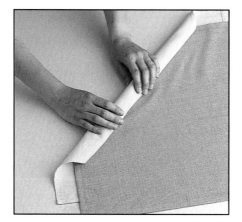

2 Starting with the corner of the V border roll up both napkins together.

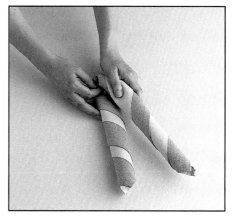

3 Loosely fold the finished roll in half and position.

Standing Christmas Tree

Ideal for the Christmas table, choose a festive-patterned napkin to make this standing fold.

1 Fold the napkin into quarters, keeping the open corners at the bottom left-hand side. Fold the napkin in half by bringing the top edge down towards you.

2 With a finger at the centre top, lift the uppermost bottom right corner and bring it over to meet the bottom left corners.

3 Carefully turn the napkin over from left to right. With a hand placed over the left-hand edge of the napkin, lift the top four bottom right corners and bring them over to meet the bottom left point.

4 Fold the napkin in half down the centre before standing it up and straightening into the four 'branches' of the finished tree.

Above: Japanese Pleat.

Decorative Pocket

This clever design makes an attractive pocket in which to place anything from eating implements to flowers.

1 Fold the napkin into quarters so that the free edges are facing away from you. Fold the first layer down so that the top corner is just above the bottom corner nearest to you.

Above: Decorative Pocket.

2 Repeat this process with the second layer, again positioning its top corner just above the one before.

3 Fold under the side corners until they just overlap at the back.

Japanese Pleat

You will need a large starched napkin for this design.

1 Fold down the edge furthest away from you by a third. Fold up the edge nearest to you in the same manner so that the napkin forms a narrow rectangle one-third its original width. With a finger at the centre top, fold down both sides towards you so that the edges meet at the centre.

2 Holding the diagonal edges, turn the napkin over so that the tip now points towards you and the top layer forms a triangle. Roll down the two extending rectangles towards you until they come just above the base of the triangle.

3 Grip the rolls firmly with two hands and turn the napkin over again so that the tip of the triangle is facing towards you. Fold the two top corners down so that their edges meet in the centre.

Below: Gathered Pleat.

Gathered Pleat

Using a simple technique and a napkin ring, create a stylish design for an informal table setting.

1 Grasp the centre of the napkin and lift it off the table so that the material hangs in soft but clearly defined folds.

2 Thread a napkin ring onto the end you are holding and slide it towards the centre. Spread out the folds to form an attractive shape.

Table Basket

A cloth napkin can become an attractive basket for breadsticks, crackers or even a dried-flower arrangement.

1 Fold down the edge furthest away from you by a third. Repeat with the edge nearest to you so that the napkin forms a narrow rectangle one-third its original width. Turn the napkin over so that the free edge is underneath and facing away from you. Fold the right edge to the centre, then fold the left edge to meet the newly formed right edge.

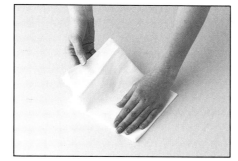

2 Pull out the first fold made in step 1.

3 Lift the top edge of the top fold and turn it down by one-third, forming a triangle at the top.

4 Repeat with the bottom edge of the top fold to form a thin flap. Press.

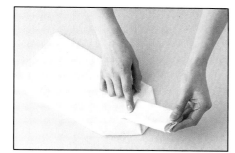

5 Fold the narrow flap to your left.

6 Now fold the wide right edge to meet the narrow left edge.

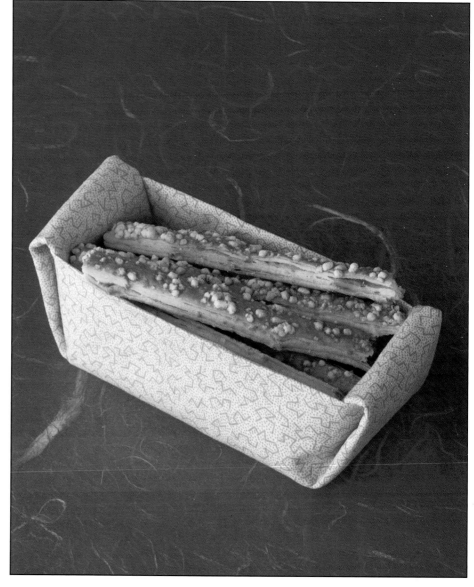

7 Follow steps 3 and 4 on the second side.

8 Fold the narrow flap on the second side to your right.

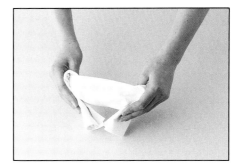

9 Holding the flaps at the centre, turn the napkin inside out. (The flaps form the lining of the rectangular basket.)

Roll-top

This is an easy napkin fold that will grace both an informal and formal table setting. The 'pockets' are ideal for presenting name cards, or perhaps a small gift on special occasions.

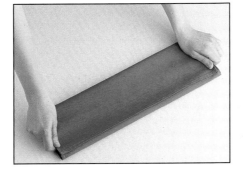

1 Fold down the edge furthest away from you by a third. Then fold up the edge nearest to you in the same manner so that the napkin forms a narrow rectangle one-third its original width.

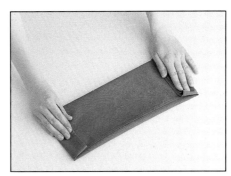

2 Fold the left and right edges over by about 5cm/2in towards the centre – adjust the size of this band according to the size of the napkin.

3 To form the first 'pocket', bring the right side of the napkin across to the left, leaving the left-hand band uncovered but its raw edge concealed.

4 Fold from the right side again, making sure that each 'pocket' measures the same width.

Valentine Heart

For this romantic shape you need a napkin that will hold a crease.

1 Fold the napkin in half bringing the top edge down towards you.

2 Fold it almost in half again bringing the bottom edges up just short of the top.

3 With a finger at the centre bottom, fold both sides up to meet in the middle.

4 Turn the napkin over, keeping the point towards you. Fold in each of the four top corners so that you make four small triangles. Reverse to finish.

Double Fan

This classic design is ideal for more formal dinners but it requires a little time to practise it. You will need a large, starched cotton napkin.

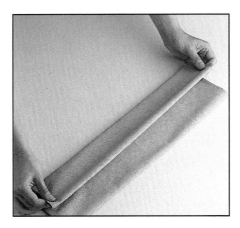

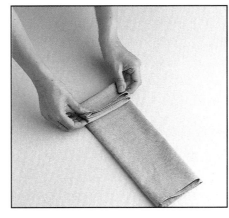

1 Fold the bottom and top edges of the napkin to meet in the centre and fold in half by bringing the bottom edge up to the top.

2 Turn the napkin so that a short edge faces you and fold it seven times to make eight accordion pleats.

3 Grasp the bottom of the pleats firmly and in between each pleat pull the layer nearest to you down to form double-layered triangles.

4 Turn the napkin round and repeat the process on the other side. Spread the folds out into the fan shape.

G.I. Cap

This children's favourite may make it difficult to stop hats being worn at the table! It works well in khaki, green or grey.

1 Bring down the edge furthest from you to fold the napkin in half. Fold the left edge into the centre.

2 Do the same with the right edge. Holding the top layer of the folded-in right edge half-way up, lift it out to the right again while holding the bottom layer in place also from half-way up. Flatten to make a triangular shape at the top.

3 Do the same with the top layer of the folded-in left side and open out in the same way. Fold both sides underneath.

4 Fold the uppermost bottom flap up to meet the bottom edge of the triangles.

5 Fold the flap again so that it half covers the triangles. Turn the napkin over and repeat the final two folds on the other flap. Hollow out and put a dent in the top crease to make the finished cap.

Sailboat

This jolly arrangement can easily be augmented with sea-related pieces, such as shells or pebbles.

1 Fold the open napkin into quarters. Keep the open corners nearest to you and fold them up to the top point.

2 With a finger placed at the top point, fold down the right and left sides by bringing each point towards you.

3 Next turn the napkin **over** and fold up the bottom point.

4 Turn the napkin over again and fold it in half backwards along the centre line. Hold the bottom firmly and open out the top layers to make the sails of the boat.

Cable Buffet

This smart design allows guests at a buffet or picnic to help themselves to napkin and cutlery all at once.

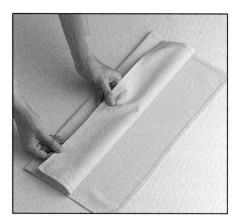

1 Fold the bottom edge of the napkin up to the top. Next fold the top layer down to meet the bottom edge.

2 Fold all the bottom layers back up a little way and turn the napkin over. To make a longer design you can turn up only the upper bottom layer as in the main picture.

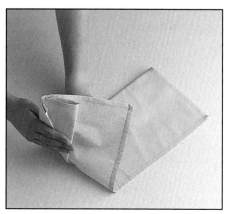

3 Bring the right side into the centre.

4 Bring the left side into the centre.

5 Tuck one half of the napkin deep into the other half locking the napkin flat. Turn over to insert cutlery into the pocket.

The Crown

The crown is one of the better-known traditional napkin folds and is often seen in restaurants. It can be used to cover a warmed bread roll at each place setting, or could hide a surprise for each guest.

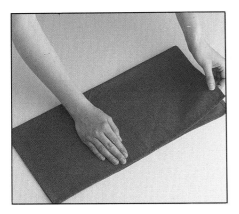

1 Fold the edge nearest to you to meet the top edge.

2 Fold the bottom right corner of the napkin up to the middle right.

3 Fold the top left corner down.

4 Turn the napkin over. Make sure that the long folded edges are directly facing you top and bottom. Fold over the top edge – the edge furthest away from you – to meet the edge nearest to you.

5 Release the second point which is still tucked under so that there are two triangles at the top.

6 Tuck the bottom left point under the edge of the right triangle. Carefully turn the napkin over and repeat the step.

7 Gently open out at the bottom to form a circle and stand the crown up.

Papillon

The brighter and more varied the patterned napkin used, the more effective your butterfly will emerge. Begin with the patterned side up.

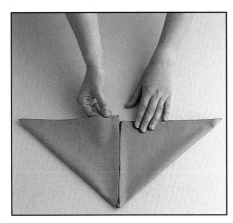

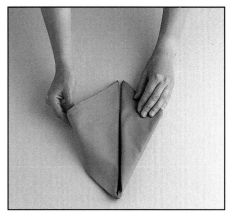

1 Fold the bottom edge of the open napkin up to the top. Fold the top left and top right corners down to meet at the bottom edge.

2 Turn the napkin over and fold in the left-hand side to make a point facing you.

3 Fold in the right-hand side in the same way. Allow the two loose layers from underneath the napkin to open out on each side.

4 Turn the napkin over so that the two loose points are facing you. Fold down the top point to tuck it into the pocket formed by the horizontal edge.

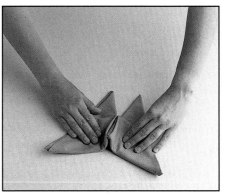

5 Placing a hand on each side of the centre, push together a small section from each side to create the butterfly's body. The upper wing tips should move slightly upwards while the tail wing tips should move apart.

Parasol

A plain or patterned napkin would be appropriate for this attractive design. You'll also need a short length of contrasting ribbon for the finishing touch.

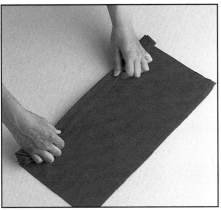

1 Make accordion pleats with the whole open napkin, beginning at the edge nearest to you.

2 Place one hand firmly over the centre of the completed pleats and bring the left edges over to the right edges, folding the napkin in half.

3 Tie a bow half-way up the pleats and then fan out the top to make the parasol.

Fanned Bow

The fanned bow is perfect for festive occasions, especially if you use a highly decorative napkin ring or shiny ribbon tied into a bow.

1 Fold the top and bottom edges of the napkin to meet in the middle to form a rectangle.

2 Rotate the napkin so that the shorter edges are facing you top and bottom. Starting at the edge nearest to you, accordian-pleat the napkin, pressing each pleat as you work.

3 Thread a wide napkin ring along to the centre of the napkin, or tie with ribbon. Fan out the pleats to make a circular bow.

Fanned Pleats

This is a quick and easy design for the beginner.

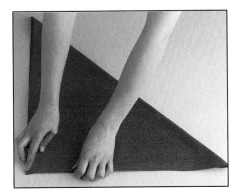

1 Fold the bottom left corner of the napkin to the top right corner.

2 Fold the resulting triangle in half, bringing the bottom right corner up to the highest point, with the top point of the napkin slightly to the left of the bottom point.

3 Fold the triangle in half again to create three points, bringing the top point up and to the right of the other two points.

4 Fold the top left corner under the napkin to give it a slender, elegant shape.

Pinwheel

An amusing party piece which will
especially appeal to children.

1 Fold the four corners into the centre.

2 Fold the top edge and the bottom edge into
the centre.

3 Bring the left and right sides into the centre.

4 Gently find each of the four loose corners at
the centre and bring them out to the side to
form four points.

5 Fold the bottom left point to the left-hand
side and the top right point to the right.

Duck Step

The duck step is a basic napkin fold that is geometrically pleasing and easy to construct.

1 Fold the bottom edge of the open napkin up to the top. Fold the napkin in half again.

2 Fold down the left side.

3 Fold down the right side to meet it in the centre. Carefully turn the napkin over.

4 Keeping hold of the centre line, fold the two sides back.

5 Separate the two square flaps and lay them flat so that the pointed centre fold stands up.

Shirt

This is a clever design which is much easier to make up than it looks!

1 Fold the four corners into the centre.

2 Next fold the top edge and the bottom edge into the centre.

3 Turn the right edge underneath to form a small hem.

4 Fold the bottom right and top right corners into the centre line to meet about the margin's width from the right edge.

5 With a hand firmly keeping the completed folds in place and a thumb at the centre of the napkin, fold out the two corners on the left.

6 Gently lift up the left edge and fold it over to the right, carefully tucking it under the points of the 'collar'.

Double Jabot

This elegant geometric design suits a smarter occasion or formal sitting.

1 Fold the napkin into quarters, keeping the open corners facing away from you. Accordion-pleat the top layer from the top point down to just below the centre line.

2 Repeat the process with the next layer finishing on the other side of the centre line.

3 Firmly holding the pleats in place, fold the right half of the napkin under the left half to form a triangle.

4 Bring the two points from the long edge together, tucking one inside the other to secure the napkin. Stand the napkin with the pleats facing outwards.

Geometric Style

Eye-catching and elegant, this is a modern design suitable for an up-beat occasion.

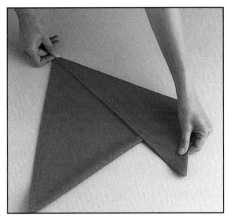

1 Starting with the corners of the open napkin top and bottom in the form of a diamond, fold the top corner down to the bottom corner. With a finger at the bottom point, fold the left side in to meet the centre line.

2 Fold the right side into the centre. Fold the left point into the centre again.

3 Fold the right point into the centre.

4 Turn the napkin over, still keeping the long point facing you. Bring the bottom point up to meet the top, folding the napkin in half.

5 Tuck the long point into the horizontal fold and reverse.

Elf's Boot

For this entertaining design use a cloth or large paper napkin. Be sure to place the finished boot the right way up to catch the diner's attention.

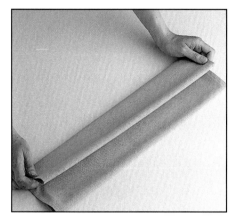

1 Fold the top and bottom edges of the napkin to meet in the middle to form a rectangle. Bring the bottom edge to meet the top edge, folding the rectangle in half.

2 With a finger at the centre bottom, fold up both sides away from you so that the edges meet in the middle.

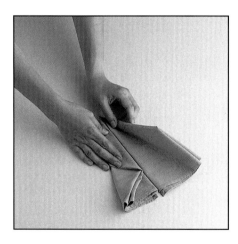

3 Fold the right and left sides closest to you into the centre to form a sharper point.

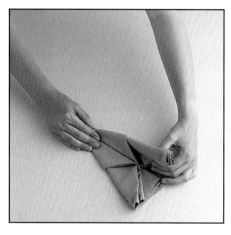

4 Fold the left side over onto the right side.

5 Move the napkin round so the bottom point now faces to your right. Fold the top left tail down towards you.

6 Fold the bottom edge of the other left tail upwards and tuck the tail securely into the pocket of the tail on the right.

Picnic Pocket

This practical idea keeps the cutlery tidy and, as it uses two napkins, provides a tablemat as well as a napkin when opened. You will need two napkins of different colours.

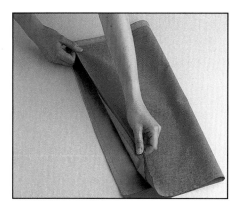

1 Place the two napkins one on top of the other with the top one slightly lower down and overlapping a little. Fold both napkins in half from left to right.

2 Lay the cutlery along the centre of the napkins and fold the side edges over to enclose it.

3 Fold the bottom edge up by about a third.

4 Bring down the top edge and tuck it into the folded bottom edge.

Bishop's Hat

This is a very traditional method of folding large dinner napkins. The proportions are important, so it may be necessary to adjust some of the folds as you work it through.

1 Starting with the corners of the open napkin top and bottom in the form of a diamond, fold the corner nearest to you to just below the corner furthest away from you to form a triangle.

2 Fold up the two corners nearest to you until the edges align.

3 Bring the newly created bottom corner up and away from you so that its top edge sits just below the first corner when folded.

4 Fold down the front edge.

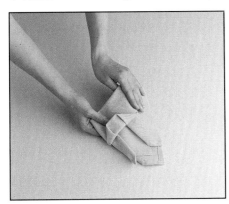

5 Bend the left and right corners backwards and interlock one half into the other to form a tube that will not spring open.

Corsage

To make this attractive design it is best to use a small napkin centred inside another one approximately one third larger. The two can then be folded together as one.

1 One by one, lift up all four points of the larger napkin and bring them neatly together.

2 Tightly holding the points together, pull the napkin along the looped edges until it flattens into a square shape when placed on its side.

3 With the open corners facing away from you, fold the right and left bottom edges of the top layer into the centre. Carefully turn the napkin over and repeat the process with the edges on this side.

4 Fold the bottom point up to meet the horizontal edges.

5 Fold the bottom half of the napkin together.

6 Holding the bottom firmly in one hand, gently spread out the open top layers.

Pure Elegance

Easy to construct, this design is ideal for both formal dining and a low-key setting.

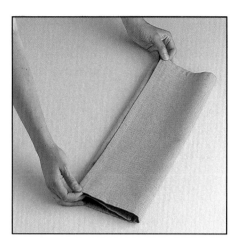

1 Fold the bottom edge up by a third and fold the top third of the napkin down over it.

2 Turn the napkin so that a short edge is nearest to you. Fold the top edge down to the centre and repeat with the bottom edge.

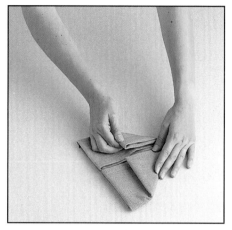

3 Fold the top left corner and bottom left corner into the centre and turn the napkin over so that the pointed edge faces towards you.

4 Bring both top points down towards each other and tuck the right point inside the pocket underneath the left point. To position, turn the napkin around and stand.

Clown's Hat

The perfect start to a birthday feast, this arrangement is seen at its best in bold or varied colours.

1 Fold the top edge of the open napkin down to meet the bottom edge. Next bring the top right corner down to the centre bottom.

2 Fold the bottom right point over to the bottom left corner.

3 Next bring the bottom right corner up to meet the top left point, folding the napkin in half diagonally.

4 Divide the eight layers on the left into two groups of four. Fold both groups back to form a small hem. Hollow out the napkin to form a cone shape.

5 Tuck the small tail into the rim of the hat to complete the fold.

Spring Time

For this slightly more complicated design a large cloth or paper napkin that will hold a crease is needed. Place the patterned or 'good' side of the napkin face down.

1 Fold the napkin in half with the fold at the top. Lift the bottom of the top layer and make accordion pleats up to the edge furthest away from you.

2 Grasp the pleats firmly and turn the napkin over so that the pleats are underneath and nearest to you. With a thumb at the centre bottom, fold up the two sides so that the pleats meet in the centre.

3 Gently turn the napkin over again from top to bottom. Fold the bottom right and left corners, tucking them into the pocket at the top point.

4 Next bring down the top point, folding the napkin in half.

5 Fold this point up again away from you but only enough so that it extends slightly beyond the top edge.

6 Lift each side corner in towards each other and tuck one inside the other.

7 Carefully turn the napkin over and fan out the pleats to finish the butterfly.

Diagonal Pockets

A smart design suitable for any occasion.
Use the pockets for decorative
accessories, such as a small flower, a
sprig of herbs or perhaps a small gift.

1 Fold the napkin into quarters, making sure
that all the open corners are at the top right-
hand side. Roll the top layer back diagonally
towards you as far as it will go.

2 Press the roll flat to form a thin band.

3 Bring the second layer back and tuck the
corner behind the first band until the folded
edge forms a parallel band the same width as
the first.

4 Repeat the process with the third layer.

5 Fold the sides under to the back to form a
neat rectangle.

Water Lily

This design requires a well-starched napkin to make the cup shape. It can be used to hold a bread roll, a small gift or seasonal decorations such as small fir cones and holly at Christmas, chocolate hearts for Valentine's Day, or a tiny posy of spring flowers.

1 Fold the corners of the napkin into the centre and press flat.

2 Repeat the process a second time.

3 Holding the centre points together, carefully turn the napkin over.

4 Fold the four corners into the centre again, but do not press.

5 Holding the centre firmly, partly pull out the previous fold from under each corner and gently pull them upward to make the petals.

6 Pull out the corners from underneath between the petals, to form the base leaves of the lily.

Bunny Rabbit

These cheeky bunny ears are the perfect table greeting for young party goers. The brighter the napkin used, the better!

1 Fold the top and bottom edges of the open napkin to meet in the centre.

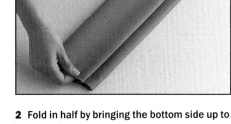

2 Fold in half by bringing the bottom side up to the top edge.

3 With a finger at the centre bottom, fold up both sides away from you so that the edges meet in the centre.

4 Fold the left and right top corners down into the centre.

5 Next fold each top outside edge into the centre making two narrow points facing away from you.

6 Holding the napkin in your left hand fold the bottom point underneath.

7 Bring the two bottom points this forms towards each other and interlock one point into the triangular pocket of the other.

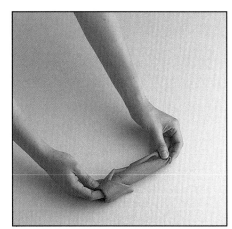

8 Using a finger inside the base of the napkin, gently shape it to make it round.

9 Carefully turn the napkin over and open out the bottom folds to make the face.

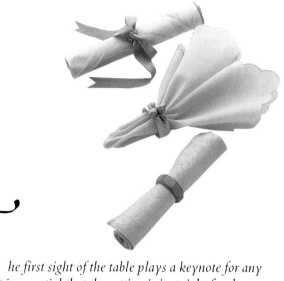

Stunning Settings

they pass through the hallway before dinner, the merest glimpse of arrangements should excite the dining instincts by hinting at the quality of the meal to come.

Whether crisp and sophisticated, softly flowing with lace and flowers, warm and homely, or refreshingly bright, the setting should confirm the guests' anticipation of the party and raise it to new levels. This section is designed to arouse your enthusiasm for scene-setting and to encourage artistic instincts. With flair and a sense of occasion you can be as individualistic as you wish, and carry off any event with outstanding success.

*T*he first sight of the table plays a keynote for any meal, so it is essential that the setting is just right for the occasion. In contemporary living-dining rooms and at buffet parties the table is on display from the moment the guests arrive; if guests happen to pass an open dining room door as

TABLE LINEN

There is an enormous variety of table linen available, most of it far removed from traditional white linen. There are no rules about what is acceptable or otherwise, the only qualification being that the choice should suit the occasion. A chequered patio cloth and bright paper napkins are not worthy of a gourmet meal of classic dishes. Conversely white damask and fine glass would seem inappropriate for a casual invitation for a snack lunch . . . .

White linen

White linen is both versatile and practical, and there is nothing quite like crisply starched, large white napkins for a dinner party table.

Heavy, white damask tablecloths and napkins are expensive but they will last for years. It is always worth looking out for good-quality second-hand linen at auctions, flea markets and in antique or junk shops – as long as the fabric is not scorched, badly marked, worn or torn, then it is a good buy.

Although spray starch is adequate for a tablecloth, the only way to get a really good finish on napkins is by starching them with traditional starch which you mix with boiling water. A good compromise, instead of soaking

the fabric in the starch solution, is to mix a small quantity according to the packet directions, then keep it in a clean plant spray bottle. Spray dry napkins and cloths before ironing, leaving the moisture to soak into the fabric for about 30 seconds. The result

is just like proper starched linen.

Although plain white linen is unsuitable for casual table settings, do not feel that it always has to form the base for extremely formal table arrangements. Introduce a contemporary air with your choice of flowers or table

White, damask table linen adds elegance to a formal dinner.

Choose brightly coloured table linen for an ethnic meal or theme party.

centrepieces; instead of traditional white candles go for coloured ones or even scented candles; or neatly roll the napkins and use colourful napkin ties or ribbons with a small flower or suitable trimming to pick up on the rest of the table decorations.

Plain and Printed Linen

Good linen in delicate pastel shades can be equally as formal as traditional white table settings. Deep colours can be more dramatic and stylish but just as formal, depending on the overall presentation. Strong colours can also make an eye-catching base for flamboyant themes, particularly when preparing an ethnic meal or for fancy dress

Table Protection

Buy a waterproof protective covering to lay on the table under the cloth. This protects the table surface from plates and glassware, and from any spills. Do not buy a cheap brand if you have a good table; it is better to spend more and know that the table is safe.

(costume) parties and buffets.

Printed and woven linen varies enormously in quality. Smart checks and stripes are useful for informal picnics, barbecues, patio meals, breakfasts and brunches.

Embroidered Linen and Lace

Colourful hand embroidery is ideal for breakfast cloths, and for table coverings for brunches, family teas and high tea. Fine work trimmed with lace and lace cloths are ideal for afternoon teas, parties in the garden, grand picnic parties and for weddings.

A garland of fresh flowers and foliage enhances an outdoor buffet table.

BUFFET SETTINGS

Buffet tables provide the perfect excuse for impressive settings, perhaps with swags of flowers or ribbons and posies as well as a large main decoration. All the food should be decorative too, and it must be arranged for ease of access when guests serve themselves.

The buffet may be placed against a wall so that guests move along in front of the table and serve themselves, or it may be situated in the middle of a room (or with space all around) so that guests move around the table. Whichever system is used, there should be an obvious starting point for serving and this is indicated by a pile of plates. On a large table, plates may be piled at both ends so that guests can work from both directions.

If the buffet is set against a wall, then the main decoration should be at the

Small garlands look pretty above entrances.

rear and positioned in the centre. If guests walk all around the table, then a centrepiece should be placed on the table.

Make sure all the dishes are easy to reach and that there are serving spoons nearby. If there is a ham or other food which needs carving, set it in a position to one side of the table so that guests do not obstruct access to other dishes while they carve. It should be someone's task to check the availability of foods, topping dishes up and tidying the buffet occasionally.

Set napkins and cutlery separately on a side table. Large paper napkins are usually used for informal buffets. If disposable plates are used, they should be sturdy and of good quality, as thin plates sag miserably and make eating difficult. Buffet-style plates are now available which include a holder for a wine glass. Alternatively, keep a large number of good-quality, large plastic plates, which are ideal for entertaining in large numbers. They are easier to rinse, stack and wash than china plates, and ideal for outdoor parties as well as for informal buffets.

Themed Settings

There are times when it is fun to abandon convention and go for something strikingly different in the way of setting arrangements. This is fine if you know the guests reasonably well, but it is not a good idea to confront business acquaintances or people you rarely meet with something out of the ordinary. Think of these setting styles as informal alternatives!

White and pastels tend to be favoured colours for table settings, but strong colours make a dramatic impact. A blue and gold setting, for example, could have a deep blue cloth and napkins, matching candles and a blue flower arrangement, such as hydrangeas, hyacinths, delphiniums, lavender or cornflowers. Wire dried autumn leaves and spray them gold, then use these with the fresh flowers.

Alternatively, try creating a lush green table using a white linen cloth as the base and limiting the other colour to green, including candles. Make a central arrangement of leaves: as well as cuttings from shrubs, take leaves from indoor plants, such as Japanese aralia and grape ivy. Create movement and interest by using leaves of different sizes and shapes.

A contrast setting could start with a black tablecloth and white dinner plates. Use black-and-white napkins, perhaps ones that have a strong, geometric pattern. To make an elongated napkin shape with points at the top and bottom, fold and press each

Combine clean lines and black and white chinaware and table linen for a strikingly modern look.

napkin into quarters, then give it a quarter turn and fold the opposite side corners over the middle so that they overlap. Press neatly and place one on each plate.

Use small white candle holders and short black candles, or small white saucers and black nightlights (votive-style candles) or small, rounded candles. Place several of these along the length of a rectangular table or around the middle of a circular table. If using white saucers, press and fold two small squares of crêpe paper to sit under the candles: one black square to go on the saucer, then a white square offset on top to go under the candle.

Any central decoration should be simple and based on white flowers with dried leaves that are wired and sprayed black.

In complete contrast, a pretty lace setting is ideal for a celebratory lunch party, for a small wedding lunch party or for a large buffet table. Lay a plain-coloured cloth or fabric over the table – pink is ideal for this theme. The colour should be reasonably strong but not garish. Lay a lace cloth over the plain cloth so that the colour shows through.

Opposite: fine lace and small posies of flowers set the scene for a celebration lunch.

Candles and candle holders come in a wide range of sizes and colours suitable for every occasion.

Lighting for Effect

Fixing on the right lighting is crucial to the success of any scene-setting plan and the results can have marked effects on your guests. Just as people will feel uncomfortable in glaringly bright surroundings more conducive to a dentist's office than to a dinner party, so they will also feel unnerved and depressed by lighting which is dim to the point of being gloomy.

For the majority of entertaining the lighting should be soft enough to make your guests look their best and to suggest that everyone ought to be relaxed. It should, however, be bright enough for people to see what is being eaten and to read the expressions across the dining table.

Candles

Candles really do give a room a pleasing glow. They should be used in conjunction with sufficient electric light to ensure that the surroundings are bright enough.

❖ Slim, tall candles are perfect for elegant dining.

❖ Chubby, bright candles are well suited to kitchen suppers and informal meals.

❖ Create different heights of light by arranging candles around the room. Place some on a fireplace hearth (set them to one side if the fire is lit, otherwise they melt and run), others on side tables and some at windowsill level.

❖ Arrange marbles or glass pebbles in a large copper or other metal bowl with nightlights. Place the bowl on a low table or footstool in a corner of the room.

❖ Wherever you place candles, make absolutely sure that they present no risk of fire and never leave lit candles unattended.

❖ Floating candles are designed for floating when alight. Select a wide-topped glass bowl and place some colourful stones, shells and artificial aquarium plants in the bowl. Float and light the candles.

❖ Combine floating candles and Japanese water flowers.

Floating candles and rosebuds in a bowl.

Set conventional place settings. Roll the napkins and tie them with satin ribbon and large bows.

Draw up the lace cloth at the corners of the table and at intervals around the edge (between place settings), then pin it in place so that it hangs in swags.

Prepare small posies of roses and tie them with flamboyant bows of satin ribbon to match the place settings. Pin the flowers on the cloth.

Arrange a large bowl of roses for the centre of the table. Make sure you have enough roses to lay one at each place

setting. Trim each stem and wrap with a leaf in a little moistened absorbent kitchen paper (paper towels). A final wrapping of foil will hold everything together and keep in the moisture. Place the roses under the bows around the napkins shortly before guests arrive.

Candles

White candles are traditional at formal dinners but this convention depends entirely on the hostess and the setting. Tall candlesticks usually have short candles and short holders take long candles. The candles may be placed in the centre of the table or at intervals along its length. If there is the space, very effective settings can be created by flouting this convention and arranging low candles or nightlights (votive-style candles) towards the table corners.

Ideas for Electric Lights

❖ Arrange fans or sunshades in front of floor spotlights to create a warm light.

❖ Make large paper lanterns and place very low-wattage bulbs in them (15 watt).

❖ Use coloured bulbs. These are especially good for lively parties,

where areas may be lit with bright red, blue or green by fitting the appropriate bulbs.

❖ Use a floor spotlight or standard spotlight to cast light from behind a large, exotic-looking indoor plant – the effect can be quite eerie.

❖ Place a low-wattage light on a windowsill to illuminate a hand-painted blind or unusual fabric.

Ribbon Rosette

This simply made old-fashioned idea is a classic trim for swathes of filmy fabric.

YOU WILL NEED: firm satin ribbon about 2.5 cm/1 in wide in two toning shades: about 1.8 m/2 yd in deeper tone and about 90 cm/1 yd in paler tone, scissors, needle and thread.

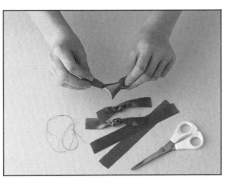

1 Cut seven 17.5 cm/7 in lengths of deeper-toned ribbon and tie a single knot fairly loosely in the middle of each.

2 Twist the ends of one of the knotted pieces of ribbon so that they lie on top of one another.

3 Twist a second piece of ribbon in the same way and hold the ends together, with the knots lying side by side.

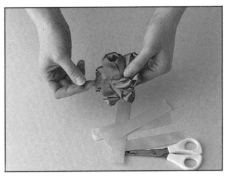

4 Continue to arrange all seven pieces of ribbon into an overlapping circle, knots evenly spaced around the edge and ends gathered in the centre. Secure the ends with a few stitches.

5 Cut five 17.5 cm/7 in lengths of paler-toned ribbon and tie in knots as before. Arrange them in the centre of the rosette and stitch in place.

6 Make a small loop of darker ribbon. Sew this in the centre of the rosette to conceal the ends and stitching, puckering it gently to make an attractive shape. Sew two long tail pieces of ribbon to the back of the rosette.

Appliqué Napkin

Appliqué in the form of flowers or fruit makes decorative corner trimmings for plain tablecloths and napkins.

YOU WILL NEED: plain coloured napkins, thin card (posterboard) for template, pencil, colourfast red fabric, green felt, scissors, iron-on interfacing, dressmaker's marking pen, red and yellow thread, needle.

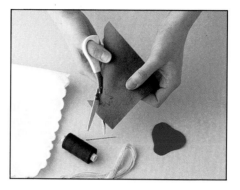

1 Transfer the strawberry shape to the red fabric and the stem shape to the green felt. You will also need to transfer the strawberry shape onto a piece of iron-on interfacing.

2 Cut around the lines using a pair of sharp scissors. Iron on the interfacing to the back of the strawberry cut-out. Mark where the seed details will go with a dressmaker's marking pen (this should be washable).

3 Tack (baste) the strawberry cut-out in place on the napkin, then stitch all around the edge using buttonhole stitch or zig-zag machine stitch. This will prevent the fabric from fraying. Tack the stem in position, then hand or machine stitch in place using a straight stitch and yellow thread. Hand stitch the seed details using the yellow thread.

Stencilled Table Linen

Wall stencils used as part of the dining room or kitchen decor can be picked up on cloths and napkins using fabric paints. Do not try to match colours, as it is unlikely you will be able to achieve the same shade with fabric paints. Select toning or contrasting colours instead. Follow the manufacturer's instructions for using fabric paint for a result which is lasting and washable.

YOU WILL NEED: plain coloured place mats and napkins; (for making stencil) paper, pencil, sticky (transparent) tape; clear acetate for stencil, waterproof black felt-tip pen, craft knife, fabric paints, paintbrush, rag.

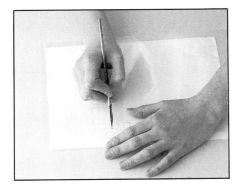

1 If you are making your own stencil, draw your design onto a sheet of paper. Place the sheet of acetate on top and tape in position to hold the sheet firmly in place. Transfer the design to the acetate using a waterproof black felt-tip pen. Cut around the outline of the stencil design with a craft knife.

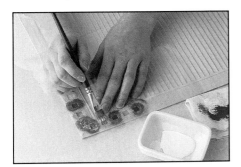

2 Load the brush with paint. Keep a rag handy for wiping excess paint from the brush. For stencilling, you should not have too much paint on the brush as this can seep beneath the stencil. Holding the stencil firmly in place, press the brush over the pattern in the stencil keeping the brush vertical. Wait for the paint to dry before applying the second colour.

3 To create a stippled effect, you will need some white or pale coloured paint and a clean brush. Lightly load the brush with paint and dab on the paint using a stabbing motion. Allow the paint to dry, then fix according to the manufacturer's instructions.

Gold Leaf Napkin Ring

Collect autumn leaves to make this elegant napkin ring. Dried beech leaves have been used here, but any medium-sized dried leaves are suitable. As an alternative, use silver spray to paint .

YOU WILL NEED: dried leaves, wire, gold spray paint, florists' dry foam (styro foam), heavy satin ribbon, needle and matching thread.

1 For each napkin ring, wire 3 dried leaves onto 20 cm/8 in wires.

2 Spray the wired leaves with gold spray paint on a well-protected work surface. Always work in a well-ventilated area. Stand each finished leaf in florists' dry foam (styro foam) to dry.

3 When the paint is dry, twist the leaves together. Arrange the leaves so that the central leaf is higher than the other two leaves. Allow about 2.5 cm/1 in of wire to remain untwisted immediately below the leaves when they have been arranged.

4 Wrap the end of the ribbon around the wire below the middle leaf, taking about 7.5 cm/3 in of the end and binding it around the twisted wire. Bind another layer of ribbon over this, then bind along the length of the wire.

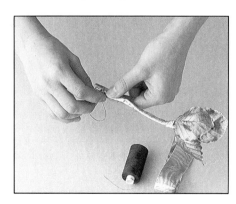

5 Stitch the ribbon in place at the end of the wire with matching thread. Trim off any protuding ends of wire. Form the ribboned wire into a ring and secure the end under the leaves with a few stitches. Gently twist the leaves in place and flatten the ring to neaten.

Greenery Chain

Make a simple chain of greenery to swag the table edge.

YOU WILL NEED: suitable foliage, plastic-covered tying wire or florists' wire, selection of herbs such as bay leaves, rosemary and thyme, needle and green thread, pins, green ribbon.

1 Join lengths of foliage together with suitable wire cut into manageable strips.

2 Wire sprigs of herbs and stitch them to the chain at intervals. Pin the chain to one corner of the table and then pin at each sprig of herbs to form swags. Trim with bows of green ribbon.

Standing Place Cards

Place cards are always laid at formal or large dinners. Simple, elegant cards are best for such occasions. Lay them in a suitable position on the setting, such as on a side plate or with the napkin.

YOU WILL NEED: card (posterboard); (for making stencil) paper, pencil, sticky (transparent) tape; craft knife, stencil or sheet of acetate, waterproof black felt-tip pen, gold paint, stencil brush, thin coloured ribbon.

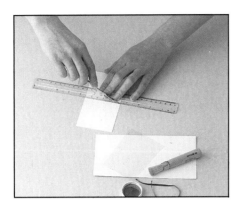

1 Cut a strip of card (posterboard) measuring 15 × 7.5 cm/6 × 3 in. Mark a fold across the centre of the card and a 2.5 cm/1 in fold at each end of the strip. Lightly score the folds with a craft knife, but be careful not to cut through the card.

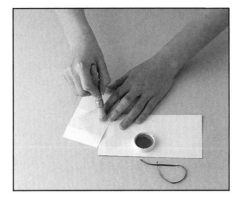

2 If you are making your own stencil, draw your design onto a sheet of paper. Place the sheet of acetate on top and tape in position to hold the sheet firmly in place. Transfer the design to the acetate using a waterproof black felt-tip pen. Cut around the outline of the design using the craft knife. Lightly load the brush with gold paint. Holding the stencil firmly in position, press the brush over the pattern in the stencil keeping the brush vertical.

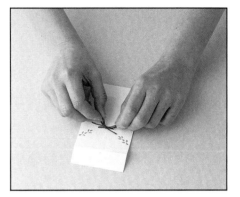

3 To attach the ribbon, mark and then cut two small slits in the card. Thread the ribbon through and tie into a bow. Trim the ends of the ribbon if necessary.

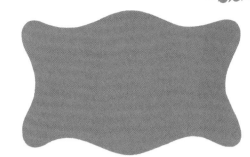

Cut-out Place Cards

Use patterned card (posterboard) for these attractive place cards: special marbled, coloured, gold or silver card is suitable.

YOU WILL NEED: plain card, patterned card, tracing paper, pencil, craft knife, glue.

1 For each place card, you will need a strip of patterned card (posterboard) measuring 20 × 10 cm/8 × 4 in. Trace the pattern for the cut-out area onto tracing paper. Using a soft pencil, shade the area underneath the tracing. Mark a fold across the centre of the card and a 2.5 cm/1 in fold at each end of the strip. Lightly score the folds with a craft knife, but do not cut through the card. Lay the tracing shaded side down on the reverse of one half of the patterned card, positioned centrally. Using a sharp pencil, follow the line of the design.

2 On a hard surface, use the craft knife to cut out the shape.

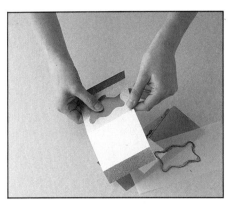

3 Push the cut-out area from the right side of the card, *not* from the back. Take care to push out any intricate designs carefully.

4 Cut out a strip of plain card measuring 9.5 × 7 cm/3¾ × 2¾ in. Stick the plain card behind the cut-out area on the patterned card with glue.

Flower Rope

A single flower rope adds decoration to an awkward panel of wall — beside a door for example. A pair looks elegant framing a fireplace. Alternatively, a series of ropes can be suspended at links in paper chains or swags of ribbon. Hung from table edges, they create a very festive atmosphere.

YOU WILL NEED: green raffia, florists' wire, florists' tape, pins, flower heads such as orchids, lilies etc, foliage such as ivy, ruscus etc, narrow and wide matching ribbon.

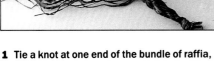

1 Tie a knot at one end of the bundle of raffia, divide the strands into three and plait (braid) loosely. Trim the end to length and secure.

2 Make a loop at one end of a length of florists' wire and wire individual ivy leaves.

3 Hold an ivy leaf and an orchid together and twist the wire around both stems. Bind both stems together with florists' tape.

4 Wire and tape together other flower heads and leaves. Insert an orchid and ivy leaf near the top of the raffia rope.

5 Insert a second wired flower head into the raffia rope below the orchid, positioning it at an attractive angle to add width.

6 Continue to add further flower heads and leaves, alternating the angles to achieve a balanced effect. Position one flower head to conceal the end of the raffia rope.

7 Wind a trail of ruscus leaves around the raffia rope, tucking it in behind the flowers. Make little long-tailed bows with narrow ribbon, and curl the ends.

8 Attach the little bows to the raffia with pins. Arrange a spray of ivy to add width at the top of the rope and wire in place. Attach a large ribbon bow at the top.

Spiky Paper Flowers

Use paper of a single colour for each bloom, or make each layer from a different shade — for example, from pink through mauve and violet to blue — for a glowing, luminous effect. Crêpe paper makes suitably chunky leaves to contrast with the delicate flowers.

YOU WILL NEED: 20 cm/8 in squares of tissue paper in flower colours and crêpe paper in green, florists' wire, small paper scissors, needle.

1 Bend a small loop in one end of a length of wire. Fold four sheets of tissue paper together into quarters. Beginning about 2.5 cm/1 in away from the central corner, cut a circle of spikes radiating out towards the outer edges of the paper.

2 Open out the folds and use a needle to make a hole through the centre. Push the straight end of the wire through the hole. Separate the tissue paper layers and rotate them slightly to stagger them.

3 Turn the flower over and gently gather the petals over the wire loop. Holding the bottom of the flower between thumb and forefinger, twist the wire two or three times around the centre of the paper to secure.

4 Fold the sheets of crêpe paper in half and cut out leaf shapes. Wire these in the same way and arrange between and around the flowers.

Felt Flower Napkin Rings

Choose fine, smooth felt and ribbon in colours to match or harmonize with your table settings.

YOU WILL NEED: (for each napkin ring) thin card (posterboard) for template, pencil, scissors, coloured and green felt, needle and thread to match, a few tiny beads; (for each felt flower) 90 cm/1 yd velvet ribbon about 1.5 cm/⅝ in wide, needle and thread to match, 20 cm/8 in plastic-covered tying wire, wire cutters.

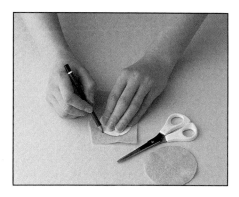

1 Cut out two circular templates, one 6.5 cm/ 2½ in in diameter and the other 4 cm/1½ in. Draw the outlines onto the felt and cut out.

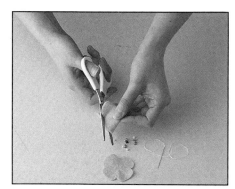

2 Fold each felt circle in quarters and cut a shallow V-shape out of the curved edge to make scalloped 'petals'.

3 Sew a tiny ring of running stitches around the centre of each flower shape, then pull the thread to pucker the centre slightly.

4 Stitch the smaller circle on top of the larger one. Sew three or four beads in the centre.

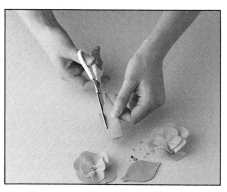

5 Cut out two leaf shapes from green felt.

6 Place the leaves on the underside of the flower and stitch.

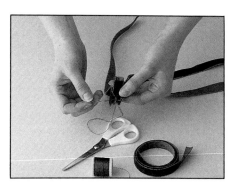

7 Cut the ribbon into three equal lengths. Stitch the ribbon lengths together at one end with matching thread.

8 Plait (braid) the ribbon neatly and not too tightly so that it forms an even band.

9 Secure the end of the plait with a few stitches and trim.

10 Run a length of plastic-covered tying wire along the back of the plait, securing it in place with a few stitches here and there.

11 Form the plait into a ring, twisting the ends of the wire together to secure. Trim off the excess wire with wire cutters. Turn the ends of the plait under and stitch together.

12 Sew the flower to the plait to cover the join.

continued . . .

continued . . .

A red poppy napkin ring will bring a splash of colour to a summer lunch table. The plaited (braided) ring is made in the same way as before.

YOU WILL NEED: (for each poppy) thin card (posterboard) for template, pencil, scissors, red felt, needle and thread to match, black haberdashers' wire for stamens; (for each napkin ring) 90 cm/1 yd velvet ribbon, 20 cm/8 in plastic-covered tying wire, wire cutters.

13 Make a card template for a three-lobed poppy shape about 7.5 cm/3 in in diameter. Draw the outline onto the felt.

14 Cut out two poppy shapes for each flower.

15 Fold the flower to find the centre and cut a tiny nick with scissors.

16 Lay the two poppy shapes together with the lobes at different angles. Shape hooked stamens using haberdashers' wire.

17 Insert the stamens into the centre of the poppy from front to back. Twist the wire around the base of the flower once or twice.

18 Stitch the wire to the base of the poppy to secure. Attach the poppy to the plaited napkin ring as before (*see step 12*).

Paper Flowers Centrepiece

Choosing tissue paper in closely graded colours for these flowers achieves the vibrant, glowing quality of real live peonies or roses. You can vary the diameter of your paper circles, with 7.5 cm/3 in being about the smallest workable size.

YOU WILL NEED: tissue paper in various colours, scissors, florists' wire, darning needle (optional), green crêpe paper.

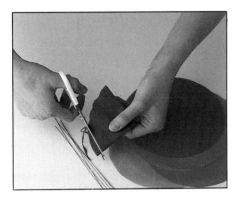

1 Cut circles of tissue paper. Fold them into quarters and flute the edges using scissors.

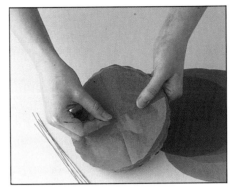

2 Stack four or six circles of tissue paper together. Bend a small loop in one end of a length of florists' wire. Use a needle to make a hole in the centre of the paper circles, then thread the straight end of the wire through from front to back.

3 Turn the paper over and gently bunch the circles up around the wire loop. Wind the wire around the base of the flower at the back to secure. Gently ease the tissue paper into attractive 'petal' shapes at the front.

4 Cut leaf shapes from crêpe paper in proportion to the flower heads. Although crêpe paper is stiffer than tissue, do not make them too large, or they will flop.

5 Bend small loops at one end of lengths of florists' wire and attach the leaves singly or in pairs. Arrange the finished flowers and leaves in a bowl.

Bonbonnières

These charming lacy holders for candies or sweets are easy to make and look pretty strewn about the table.

YOU WILL NEED: for each holder a circle of tulle or lace about 15 cm/6 in in diameter plus trimming, needle and thread, ribbons, sugared almonds, pastel-coloured mints, cashews, mixed nuts or other confectionery.

1 Hem the edge of the fabric circle and trim it with lace, if you like.

2 Place a few sugared almonds or other confectionery in the centre of the circle of fabric. Tie up the bonbonnière into a neat bundle with fine satin ribbon. Attach a small name tag if you like and place the bonbonnières in position on the table.

Ribbon Candle Holder Trims

Simple and quick to conjure up, these pretty ribbon trims can be made to echo a special colour scheme. Remember: lit candles should never be left unattended, and make sure they do not burn to within reach of the candle holder trims.

YOU WILL NEED: wide-topped candle holders, fine garden or florists' wire, ribbon, scissors, candles, herbs or other greenery (optional).

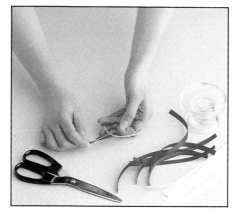

1 Wind two or three thicknesses of wire into a ring just large enough to fit neatly inside the top of each candle holder. Twist the ends of the wire around the ring to secure.

2 Cut the ribbon into pieces about 15 cm/6 in long. Double a length of ribbon and insert the loop under the wire.

3 Pass the ends of the ribbon through the loop and tighten to knot it on the wire.

4 Continue knotting ribbon around the wire ring until the wire is completely covered.

5 Trim the ends of the ribbon to neaten, then repeat for the second ring. Place the wire rings in the candle holders. Decorate with herbs or other greenery if wished.

Valentine's Heart

Set hearts a-flutter with this red and white ribbon-covered decoration. Choose ribbons in pattern variations on your chosen colour scheme. Alternatively, use patterned and plain fabric, carefully cut into ribbon strips.

YOU WILL NEED: 50—60 cm/20—24 in thick plastic-covered garden wire, piece of florists' wire, about 7.5 m/8 yd ribbon 2.5 cm/1 in wide, about 0.5 m/½ yd ribbon 5 cm/2 in wide, scissors, needle and thread.

1 Twist the thick wire into a heart shape and bind the two ends together securely in the centre with florists' wire. Cut the narrower ribbon into approximately 15 cm/6 in lengths.

2 Double a length of ribbon and knot it over the wire. Repeat with more ribbon knots until the wire is completely covered.

3 Fold a 20 cm/8 in length of wider ribbon to make a bow loop and hold it together with a couple of stitches.

4 Loop the rest of the wider ribbon around the middle of the bow loop and shape into a pair of tails. Secure with a stitch or two.

5 Attach the bow at the centre of the heart to cover the florists' wire. Trim the ends of the ribbon into swallowtail shapes.

Valentine's Day Dinner Party

❖ Cut heart-shaped invitations and send them to good friends who will want to share Valentine's Day night as a foursome.

❖ The menu is light and pink champagne is the perfect drink!

❖ The idea of the menu is that it can be romantic for two, or something of a fun occasion for four. Take the "pink heart" theme to extremes by fixing a pink cocktail before dinner – a mixture of Angostura Bitters, gin and tonic. It can be fun to go completely over the top by preparing heart-shaped cheese biscuits (crackers) too!

Woven Heart Bonbon Holder

The symbolic interlacing in this pretty heart-shaped pouch makes it appropriate as a Valentine's Day gift as well as for an engagement announcement. Two colours underline this theme, but the result is attractive when card (posterboard) of just one colour is used.

YOU WILL NEED: card, pencil, ruler, scissors, glue, ribbon, shredded tissue paper, bonbons.

1 Measure and draw a 23 × 15 cm/9 × 6 in oblong shape on two different coloured pieces of card (posterboard).

2 Cut out the oblongs.

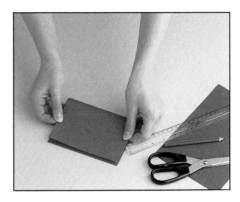

3 Fold each piece of card in half widthways.

4 Lay the two pieces of card together in an L-shape, with folded sides facing away from you, to form a square where they overlap, and lightly mark in pencil the central point at the top edge where they meet.

5 Along one short edge of each piece of folded card, measure and mark in pencil two equally spaced 11.5 cm/4½ in lines.

6 Cut along the marked lines through both layers of card.

7 Mark smooth curves at each end of the uncut short side of each folded piece of card and cut off the corners to make the rounded top edges of the heart.

8 Place the two pieces of card side by side, with the folds at right angles to each other and facing outwards. Weave the first strip from the right-hand piece over the nearest strip from the left-hand piece, through the second strip and over the third.

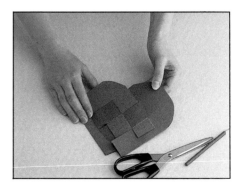

9 Weave the second strip in the same way as the first, alternating the over and under sequence. Weave the third strip in the same way as the first.

10 Turn the heart over and weave the strips on the underside in the same way to make a pouch shape at the top of the heart.

11 Dab a little glue under the ends of the strips and stick each one down.

12 Stick lengths of ribbon to the centre back and centre front of the heart, on the inside.

13 Pack some shredded tissue paper into the heart before loosely filling with bonbons.

14 Tie the ribbons in a bow to close the packet and hold the bonbons inside.

Silk Posy

The flowers for this posy should include one outstanding 'star', such as a full-blown rose, and a selection of smaller blooms and buds. Leaves and fine composite flower heads provide a delicate background and infilling to the composition.

YOU WILL NEED: florists' paper ribbon, silk and/or dried flowers and leaves, fine florists' wire, florists' tape, scissors.

1 Carefully tear off a narrow strip of ribbon.

2 Loop the wide length of ribbon once to form a bow shape. Pinch the ribbon together in the centre gently without creasing it too much.

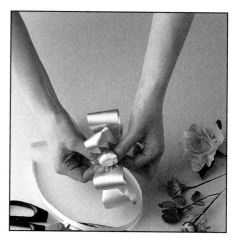

3 Loop the ribbon again to make a double bow. One end of the ribbon will be in the centre front: loop this end around into a small, neat circle to finish off the bow. Hold it in place with the thumb.

4 Still holding the bow with one hand, thread the narrow strip of ribbon through the central loop of the bow.

5 Turn the bow over and tie the narrow ribbon firmly to secure the bow. Don't trim the ends.

6 Attach individual flowers to fine florists' wire. Wire the smaller flowers and buds together in clusters. Tape the wired stems and add leaves.

7 Tie on a strip of ribbon for the tails of the bow. Measure the flowers against the bow when forming the posy. Make the posy almost as wide as the bow at the top, tapering gracefully below. When the shape is right, wire the flowers together firmly and use the ends of narrow ribbon to tie them firmly at the back of the bow. Make a hanging loop from the narrow ribbon, then trim off any excess.

Pomander Decorations

Orange and lemon pomanders are pretty hung around the kitchen suspended from ribbon, or arranged in a bowl as a table centrepiece. Stud them all over with cloves to keep longer.

YOU WILL NEED: oranges and lemons, soft pencil, cloves, ribbon, pins.

1 Using a soft pencil, lightly mark segments lengthways on the fruit. Press the cloves along the pencilled lines, spacing them evenly.

2 Take a length of ribbon and wrap it lengthways on the fruit, positioning it between two rows of cloves. Tie it off at one end. Repeat, tying off the second ribbon in the same position as the first.

3 Take a separate piece of ribbon and thread it under the knot of the ribbon on the fruit. Tie it into a bow and insert a pin through the ribbon and into the fruit to hold it in place. The pin may be disguised by folding one loose end of the ribbon over the join and tucking it under.

Ribbon Rosebuds

Tiny ribbon rosebuds make charming decorations for all sorts of occasions, from weddings to christenings. They also look good as trimmings for table linen and in guest rooms.

YOU WILL NEED: green and yellow satin ribbon, needle and matching thread, scissors, florists' wire.

1 Curl the end of a long piece of ribbon into a tight roll.

2 Secure one end of the roll with a small stitch of matching thread.

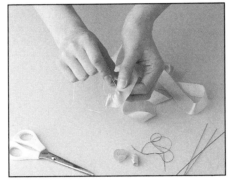

3 Make tiny running stitches along the edge of the ribbon to gather it slightly.

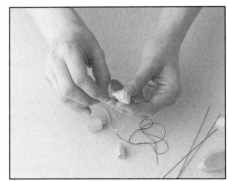

4 Roll the ribbon up, tightly at first and then more loosely until the rosebud is the required size. Trim away surplus ribbon, then turn the raw edge under to prevent fraying and secure with a tiny stitch.

5 Stitch the roses in small clusters to lengths of florists' wire.

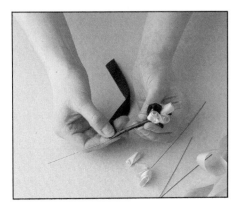

6 Using green thread, stitch a few loops of green ribbon around the base of the rosebuds. Wind the ribbon around the wire and secure with a stitch.

Wheat Napkin Ring

This simple napkin ring adds a rustic charm to Thanksgiving, harvest suppers or any mealtime occasion when the nights are drawing in.

YOU WILL NEED: (for each ring) three small dried leaves, fine florists' wire, paper varnish and brush, three ears of wheat with 25 cm/10 in stems attached, three 25 cm/10 in lengths of stalk without heads, hot water, ribbon.

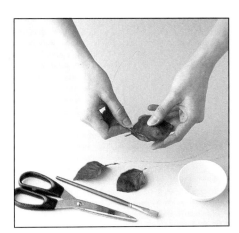

1 Wire the stems of the dried leaves.

2 Paint the leaves with paper varnish and allow to dry.

3 Soak the wheat stalks for about 30 minutes in very hot water to soften them. Drain and then blot dry.

4 Very gently insert a length of florists' wire into each stalk, leaving a little wire protruding at the ends.

5 Attach a leaf to the base of each wheat ear, then wire in one of the headless stalks.

6 Plait (braid) the wheat stalks together as evenly as possible.

7 Twist the plait into a ring and wire in place. Neaten the end.

8 Tie a ribbon bow below the leaves and wheat ears to conceal the join.

Dried-flower Posy

An elegant silk bow is the keynote of this dome-shaped arrangement which makes the perfect adornment for any table. Choose flowers in rich tapestry tones to harmonize with the bow.

YOU WILL NEED: silk fabric, needle and matching thread, hemisphere of florists' dry foam (styro foam), florists' wire, about 12 main dried flowers, other smaller flowers and sprays, dried reindeer moss.

3 Stand back and consider the arrangement before adding final blossoms all around to balance and soften the shape.

1 Make a large bow of silk fabric and sew a narrow hanging loop to the back. Thread a length of florists' wire through the back of the bow, twist the ends together and stick it into the foam. Begin the arrangement from the bow by inserting some smaller blossoms and moss.

2 Build up the arrangement around the edges of the foam. Anchor tufts of moss with loops of wire. Distribute the main deep-coloured blooms evenly around the hemisphere. Gradually work in towards the centre, interspersing the main blooms and moss with smaller flowers and sprays.

Holly Table Arrangement

Use an attractive bowl or pot as the base for the arrangement. Poinsettia flowers, real or silk, make an attractive decoration at the base to cover the gravel.

YOU WILL NEED: a length of garden cane (bamboo stake), a dry florists' foam (styro foam) sphere, sticky (transparent) tape, florists' ribbon, scissors, small block of dry florists' foam, container, gravel, florists' wire, holly sprigs, artificial florists' pine sprigs, ivy leaves, real or silk poinsettias, narrow satin ribbon (optional), wide decorative ribbon for container.

1 Insert one end of a length of garden cane (bamboo stake) into the foam sphere.

2 Tape the end of a piece of florists' ribbon to the top of the cane, then wrap ribbon around the entire length. Secure with tape at the base.

3 Insert the end of the garden cane into a piece of dry foam (styro foam) placed in a decorative container. Fill with gravel.

4 Make a loop at one end of a length of florists' wire and wire individual holly sprigs. Also wire artificial florists' pine sprigs.

5 Push the wired stems into the foam to cover it evenly. Add wired individual ivy leaves to fill any gaps.

6 Insert the poinsettias into the gravel to disguise the pebbles. Tie a wide ribbon around the container. If liked, a few red ribbon bows can be added to the holly arrangement.

Bowl of Candles

Make a bowl of candles for the centrepiece of an informal supper party. Use a bowl which has a lovely rim or highly decorated exterior. Colourful stones or coloured glass pebbles could also be used to cover the sand.

YOU WILL NEED: a suitable bowl, sand, coloured candles in different sizes, a range of sea shells.

1 Fill the bowl two-thirds full with clean sand. The sand must be deep enough to support the candles. Place a tall candle securely in the middle of the bowl.

2 Place shorter candles around the central candle. Depending on the size of the bowl, you may have room for several rows of candles, with each row getting smaller towards the edge of the bowl.

3 Once the candles are in position, arrange a variety of pretty shells around them to cover the sand completely.

Winter Candles

This seasonal arrangement of pine cones and nuts can be transformed into a Christmas centrepiece with a coating of gold or silver spray paint. Tie a gold or silver ribbon around the outer rim of the bowl and finish with a bow.

YOU WILL NEED: a suitable bowl, sand, candles of different sizes, pine cones, selection of nuts.

NOTE: Never leave candles unattended and make sure they do not burn down too close to any decorative arrangements.

1 Fill the bowl two-thirds full with clean sand. The sand must be deep enough to support the candles. Place a tall candle in the middle of the bowl, and arrange smaller ones around it.

2 Once the candles are in position, arrange the pine cones on the sand.

3 Fill any gaps left by the pine cones on the sand with nuts.

Cocktail Tray

Give a plain or scratched old tray a face-lift with a cut-out paper design. The instructions here show a sophisticated geometric pattern for an oval tray, but the principle can be adapted to any shape of tray. You can trim the tray just to fit it in with a particular party theme, but using strong glue and two coats of clear polyurethane varnish will effect a permanent transformation.

YOU WILL NEED: tray, paper for templates, pencil, scissors, ruler, gold and silver good-quality stiff paper, glue, black good-quality stiff paper or tape, paper or polyurethane varnish (optional).

1 For the first template, take a sheet of paper large enough to cover the base of the tray. Stand the tray on the paper and draw around the base.

2 Cut out the tray shape. Check that it fits the tray bottom accurately.

3 Fold the template in half lengthways, then open it out again. Make folds across both ends of the paper as shown, then open them out.

4 Fold the template in half again along the first fold. Fold the curved ends of the paper back towards the centre, using the second fold as a guide, then pleat the folded ends as shown to make three wedge-shaped creases at each end of the template.

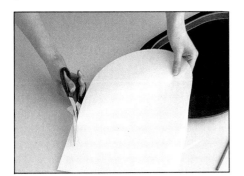

5 Open out the template. Use a ruler and sharp pencil to draw lines along each of the fold marks. Draw the diamond shape and triangles in the middle of the tray. Make a second identical template.

6 Turn one template over and spread glue evenly on the unmarked side. Stick it down smoothly onto the tray so that the pencil marks are on top.

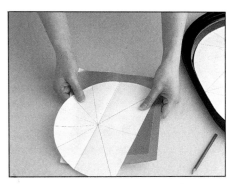

7 Fold and then cut the second template in half. You will need this quantity of gold and of silver paper, but do not yet cut out the individual segments.

8 Mark on both templates which segments are to be gold and which are to be silver: the two colours alternate.

9 Cut apart the sections of the second template, then cut out the corresponding pieces of gold and silver paper.

10 Lay the pieces of gold and silver paper in position on the tray, following the marks on the template. Check that they all fit before applying any glue.

11 Glue the pieces of paper in position on the tray. (The kind of glue depends on how lasting you want the decoration to be.)

12 Cut narrow strips of black paper or tape to cover the joins between the different papers. Remember to cut the ends at angles where they join other black strips and to fit the edges of the tray neatly. Carefully glue the strips over the joins.

13 Coat the finished tray with paper varnish or two coats of clear polyurethane varnish, allowing the varnish to dry thoroughly between coats and before use.

Decorative Candle Wreath

Highlighted with touches of gold, natural colours and forms glow appealingly in this table centrepiece. Remember that the lit candles should never be left unattended, and make sure they do not burn down to within reach of the wreath.

YOU WILL NEED: dry foam (styro foam) ring, four candles, florists' wire, nuts, strong glue, small fir cones, dried hydrangea head, tiny gold baubles, berries or rose hips.

1 Twist two lengths of wire around the base of each candle, leaving double ends of wire projecting downwards. Spear these wires firmly into the foam ring, spacing the candles evenly.

2 Stick nuts to the foam in attractive groups.

3 Add clusters of fir cones between the nuts. Twist wire around the base of cones that have no stalks, or use strong glue to stick them in place.

4 Fill spaces in the ring with hydrangea florets (flowerets), sticking them in place with glue. Add baubles and berries as finishing touches.

NOTE: Never leave lit candles unattended, and never allow candles to burn down too close to the decorations.

Yellow and Peach Table Centrepiece

When working on a table arrangement to be seen from all sides, it's a good idea to keep viewing it from different angles to make sure that it looks equally good all round. This oval arrangement is asymmetrical but evenly balanced.

YOU WILL NEED: a container, a block of wet florists' foam, flowers and foliage (wired as necessary), ribbon loops.

1 Establish the overall width and length of the arrangement using sprays of leaves as a foundation. Next place three or five flower sprays at key points to create the outline shape and height.

2 Fill in the central shape using clustered heads of tiny flowers.

3 Position larger shapely flower heads to add drama, maintaining the overall shape. Insert smaller flowers and ribbon bows to finish.

INDEX

Step-by-step projects are written in *italic*.